Especially for

_____

From

_____

Date

_____

Promises
to Bless Your Heart

Inspiration for a Blessed Life

BARBOUR
PUBLISHING

© 2011 by Barbour Publishing, Inc.

ISBN 978-1-61626-166-5

Devotional selections from *365 Daily Whispers of Wisdom for Busy Women*, published by Barbour Publishing, Inc.

Prayers by Donna K. Maltese are from *Power Prayers to Start Your Day*, published by Barbour Publishing, Inc. Prayers by Rachel Quillin are from *Power Prayers for Mothers*, published by Barbour Publishing, Inc. Prayers by Jackie M. Johnson are from *Power Prayers for Women*, published by Barbour Publishing, Inc.

Published by Barbour Publishing, Inc., P.O. Box 719, Uhrichsville, Ohio 44683, www.barbourbooks.com

Our mission is to publish and distribute inspirational products offering exceptional value and biblical encouragement to the masses.

Printed in China.

Contents

Bless Your Heart!

God's blessing makes life rich;
nothing we do can improve on God.

PROVERBS 10:22 MSG

No matter what the days may bring,
God will always be there to fill your cup to
overflowing with His blessings. Ask Him to
bless your heart today. . . . He won't let you
down. That's a promise you can count on!

Promise of Assurance

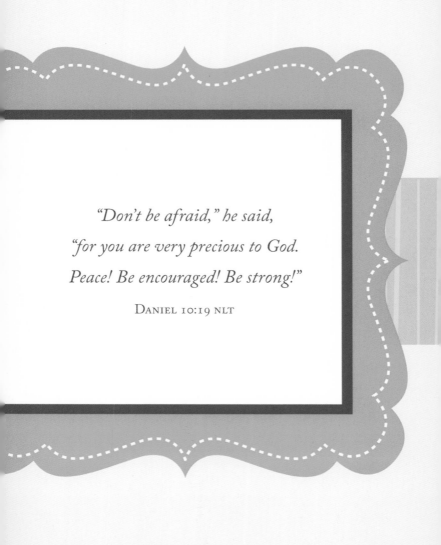

"Don't be afraid," he said,
"for you are very precious to God.
Peace! Be encouraged! Be strong!"

Daniel 10:19 nlt

Blessed Assurance

Daniel was a man of strength and character. Taken to the conquering enemy's land, he remained faithful to God, refusing to yield to the pressures around him. He insisted on eating vegetables instead of the rich food of the king, and God blessed him with good health. Daniel would not bow down and pray to King Darius but continued praying to his God instead. And when Daniel was thrown into the den of lions as punishment, God protected him by closing the lions' mouths.

God continually blessed Daniel with the favor of the king and with the ability to see and interpret visions. Nevertheless, during Daniel's last recorded vision, he confessed that he was afraid and weak. He nearly fainted but was revived and comforted with the strengthening words above.

Faith and commitment to God are as challenging today as they were when Daniel lived. Temptation surrounds us, and even when we obey the Word of God and stand firm, we sometimes grow weak and afraid. Coming face-to-face with the power of God may be even more overwhelming than dealing with the pressures of life. These words spoken to Daniel so long ago are words that still apply to us today. Are you afraid, troubled, or weak? Do not fear. Be at peace. Take heart and be strong. You are deeply loved by God!

—*Mandy Nydegger*

God wants nothing from us except our needs,
and these furnish Him with room to display His
bounty when He supplies them freely. . . .
Not what I have but what I do not have is the
first point of contact between my soul and God.

<small>CHARLES H. SPURGEON</small>

A Daily Benediction

May You walk down the road with me today.
May You shower my path with Your many blessings.
May You keep me from danger. May Your light
keep me from the darkness surrounding me.
May You give me grace and peace and strength for the
day. May You give me someone to bless as You
have blessed me. May You be there, waiting for
me at the end of the day, with a good word to
calm my spirit as I rest in Your arms.

—Donna K. Maltese

Am I a God at hand, saith the Lord,

and not a God afar off? . . .

Do not I fill heaven and earth?

JEREMIAH 23:23–24 KJV

Infinite and Personal

Back in the 1950s, the Union of Soviet Socialist Republics sent up its first satellite, *Sputnik*. At that time, communism held Russia in its tightfisted grip. Everyone who was anyone in the USSR was a communist and an atheist. Not long after *Sputnik*, the Russian cosmonauts circled planet Earth. After their return to earth, one cosmonaut made this announcement to the world: "I saw no God anywhere."

When U.S. astronauts finally made it into space some months later, one remarked, "I saw God everywhere!"

Our worldview determines the way we see reality. The cosmonaut didn't expect to see God, and he didn't. The astronaut didn't see anything more or less than his Russian counterpart, but he came away with an entirely different response. God says that He is both close at hand and over all there is. The late theologian and philosopher Francis Schaeffer called Him the infinite-personal God.

Whether your day is crumbling around you or is the best day you have ever had, do you see God in it? If the "sky is falling" or the sun is shining, do you still recognize the One who orders all the planets and all your days? Whether we see Him or not, God tells us He is there. And He's here, too—in the good times and bad.

—*Katherine Douglas*

God moves in a mysterious way

His wonders to perform;

He plants His footsteps in the sea,

And rides upon the storm.

WILLIAM COWPER

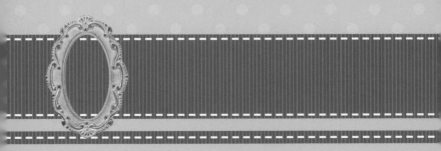

The Right Focus

Lord, I am thirsty, parched with the demands
of this world. I am in want in so many ways.
Help me not to focus on what I don't have, but
to focus on You and the blessings that You have
prepared for me. . . . Pour out Your Spirit upon
me now. Fill me with Your presence. Give me
hope for this day. I anticipate blessings waiting
around every corner. Thank You, Lord, for taking
such good care of me. You, my Savior, are the
greatest blessing of all!

—*Donna K. Maltese*

"For I will pour out water to quench your thirst and to irrigate your parched fields. And I will pour out my Spirit on your descendants, and my blessing on your children."

ISAIAH 44:3 NLT

Promise of Blessing

And Sarah said, "God has made me laugh,

and all who hear will laugh with me."

Contagious Laughter

Nothing brings more joy to our hearts than when God blesses our lives. Like Sarah, we may at first laugh with disbelief when God promises us our heart's desire. For some reason, we doubt that He can do what we deem impossible. Yet God asks us, as He did Sarah, "Is anything too hard for the LORD?" (Genesis 18:14 NIV).

Then when the blessings shower down upon us, we overflow with joy. Everything seems bright and right with the world. With God, the impossible has become a reality. We bubble over with laughter, and when we laugh, the world laughs with us! It's contagious!

When Satan bombards us with lies—"God's not real"; "You'll never get that job"; "Mr. Right? He'll never come along"—it's time to look back at God's Word and remember Sarah. Embed in your mind the truth that with God, nothing is impossible (see Matthew 19:26). And then, in the midst of the storm, in the darkness of night, in the crux of the trial, laugh, letting the joy of God's truth be your strength.

—*Donna K. Maltese*

Trust in your Redeemer's strength. . .exercise what faith you have, and by and by He shall rise upon you with healing beneath His wings. Go from faith to faith and you shall receive blessing upon blessing.

CHARLES H. SPURGEON

Heavenly Blessings

Because I am united with Your Son, who gave His life
so that we could live, You have blessed me with every
spiritual blessing. Here I sit, at my Savior's knee,
His hand upon my head. I am at peace. I am blessed.
I am in the heavenly realms. Here, nothing can harm me,
for He has blessed me beyond measure. Lord,
my cup runneth over with love for You!

—*Donna K. Maltese*

Blessed be the Lord, who daily loadeth us with benefits, even the God of our salvation.

One Day at a Time

There's a reason why the Lord's Prayer teaches us to ask for daily bread. We tend to forget about yesterday's provision in the crunch of today's needs. God calls us to a childlike faith, one that basks in the provisions of the moment and forgets yesterday's disappointments and tomorrow's worries.

Think about small children. A toddler may cry when another child knocks him down and takes away his ball. The tears disappear when his mother hugs him and gives him a kiss. His joy in the expression of his mother's love obliterates his disappointment about the toy. Later he returns to the ball with fresh enthusiasm. He lives in the moment.

God always provides for us. Benefits overflow the shopping carts of our lives every day. But He only gives us what we need for today, not for tomorrow. He knows that we need those benefits like a daily vitamin. By tomorrow, even later today, we may forget all that God has done for us. The Bible verse that spoke to us this morning feels empty by afternoon.

God gives us blessings every day so that we still have what we need after we have spent ourselves on life's disappointments.

—*Darlene Franklin*

The sun. . .in its full glory,
either at rising or setting—
this, and many other like blessings we
enjoy daily; and for the most of them,
because they are so common, most men
forget to pay their praises.
But let not us.

IZAAK WALTON

Praise Ye the Lord

I praise God from whom all blessings flow.
You bless us beyond measure, we the sheep of Your
pasture. You give us green meadows in which to lie
down, calm waters to give us rest. You forgive us our
sins. You love us beyond measure. There is no greater
blessing than Your presence in my life, than Your
desire to hear of all my troubles, cares, and woes.
You are here to lift the burden from my shoulders
and shower blessings down upon me. I praise the
name of Jesus in whom I cannot but trust.

—*Donna K. Maltese*

May the peoples praise you, O God;

may all the peoples praise you.

Then the land will yield its harvest,

and God, our God, will bless us.

PSALM 67:5–6 NIV

Promise of God's Love

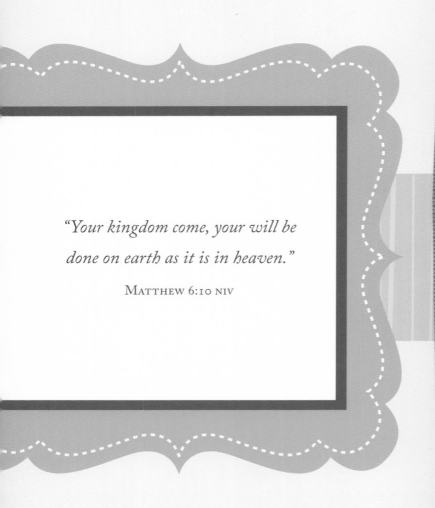

"Your kingdom come, your will be done on earth as it is in heaven."

Matthew 6:10 niv

Thy Will Be Done

We pray it. We say it. But do we really mean that we want God's will to be done on earth as it is in heaven? Submitting to God's will is difficult. Jesus struggled with submission in the Garden of Gethsemane. We wrestle with it most days. Unfortunately, most of us assume that we know best. We want to call the shots and be in control. But following God's path requires trusting Him, not ourselves.

Many times submitting to God's will requires letting go of something we covet. We may be called to walk away from a relationship, a job, or a material possession. At other times God may ask us to journey down a path we would not have chosen. Venturing out of our comfort zone or experiencing hardship is not our desire.

Embracing God's love enables us to submit to His will. God not only loves us immensely, but He desires to bless us abundantly. However, from our human perspective, those spiritual blessings may be disguised. That is why we must cling to truth. We must trust that God's ways are higher than ours. We must believe that His will is perfect. We must hold fast to His love. As we do, He imparts peace to our hearts, and we are able to say with conviction, "Your will be done."

—*Julie Rayburn*

Let Jesus be in your heart,

Eternity in your spirit,

The world under your feet,

The will of God in your actions.

And let the love of God shine forth from you.

CATHERINE OF GENOA

Loved Now and Forever

No matter what happens, Lord, I cannot be separated from You and Your love. Oh, what that means to me! Fill me with the love that never ends. May it flow through me and reach those I meet this day. May my future be filled with blessing upon blessing, and may I praise You today and in the days to come.

—*Donna K. Maltese*

"And when you look up to the sky and see the sun, the moon and the stars—all the heavenly array—do not be enticed into bowing down to them and worshiping things the Lord your God has apportioned to all the nations under heaven."

DEUTERONOMY 4:19 NIV

Created vs. Creator

The sun, moon, and stars are not to guide our lives, regardless of the power their light seems to have over us or the horoscopes people have concocted. God placed those lights in the sky with the touch of His little finger and could turn them off again, if He so chose, with less effort than it would take to flip a switch. They are beautiful creations, but they do not compare with the Creator!

Once in a while nature takes our breath away. We marvel at snowcapped mountains or get caught up in the colors of a sunset. Our heavenly Father is like a loving parent on Christmas Eve who arranges gifts beneath the tree, anticipating the joy those gifts will bring to His children.

When God fills the sky with a gorgeous sunset, it is not just about the colors and the beauty. Those colors reflect His love. He paints each stroke, each tiny detail, and mixes purples with pinks and yellows so that you might *look up*! When you look up to find the bright lights that govern our days and nights, or the next time you see a sunset, remember the Creator and give Him glory.

—*Emily Biggers*

God's gifts put man's best dreams to shame.

ELIZABETH BARRETT BROWNING

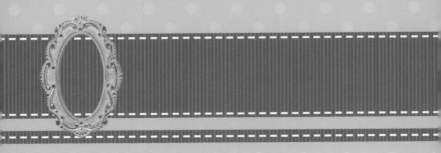

Living a Life of Love

Lord, I want to live a life of love! Show me what true love is—Your love—so I can receive it and give it away to others. Teach me to care for my neighbor as I would care for myself. Let love be my motivation for action. Help me to speak kind, encouraging words and to bless others with my actions, as well. I thank You that Your amazing, unconditional, accepting love sustains me.

—*Jackie M. Johnson*

"A new command I give you: Love one another.

As I have loved you, so you must love one another."

JOHN 13:34 NIV

Promise of God's Plan

O Lord, you are my God; I will exalt you and praise your name, for in perfect faithfulness you have done marvelous things, things planned long ago.

ISAIAH 25:1 NIV

Marvelous Plans

God had marvelous plans for the children of Israel, and they were blessed by God. God sent bread from heaven each morning in the form of manna while Israel wandered in the wilderness. When the people complained they had no meat, God sent quail. When the people complained they had no water, God gave water from a rock.

Amazingly, everything the people needed, God provided in the wilderness over and over again. Yet when they came to the Promised Land, only Joshua and Caleb believed that God would help them conquer the land. Everyone else was afraid and complained—again. Because of their faith, Joshua and Caleb were the only ones God allowed to move into the Promised Land.

God has a "promised land" for us all—a marvelous plan for our lives. Recount and record His faithfulness in your life in the past, because God has already demonstrated His marvelous plans to you in so many ways. Then prayerfully anticipate the future journey with Him. Keep a record of God's marvelous plans in a journal as He unfolds them day by day. You will find God to be faithful in the smallest aspects of your life and oh so worthy of your trust.

—June Hetzel

God wishes to be seen, and He wishes to
be sought, and He wishes to be expected,
and He wishes to be trusted.

JULIAN OF NORWICH

God Has Good Plans for Me

Lord, I am glad to know that You have plans for me—
because the future is so unclear in my mind.
You desire to prosper, not to harm, me. As the giver of all
good gifts, You wrap up hope and a future as my present.
I call upon You, Lord, knowing that You always listen.
I seek You with all my heart, Lord, and look forward with
expectant hope to good things to come.

—Jackie M. Johnson

For you created my inmost being;

you knit me together in my mother's womb.

PSALM 139:13 NIV

Creation's Praise

God didn't spend seven days creating things and then put His creation abilities on the shelf. He is continually creating wonderful things for His people. He created each of us with a special design in mind. Nothing about us is hidden from Him—the good parts or the bad.

Before you had a thought or moved a muscle, God was working out a plan for your existence. Maybe He gave you brown hair and a sweet smile or good genes for a long life. Maybe He gave you dark hair and artistic abilities. Perhaps He gave you a musical voice that worships Him daily in song. Whatever His gifts, He designed them just for you, to bring ministry to His hurting world.

When we look at the seven days of Creation, let's thank God that He didn't set things working and then walk away. Adam and Eve were important to Him, but so are we. He has personally created everything in this wonderful world—including us.

Do we need any more reason to praise the Lord who brought into existence every fiber of our beings?

—Pamela McQuade

We do not need to search for heaven, over here or over there, in order to find our eternal Father. In fact, we do not even need to speak out loud, for though we speak in the smallest whisper or the most fleeting thought, He is close enough to hear us.

TERESA OF AVILA

God Finishes What He Starts

Lord, I am so glad You finish what You start in us.
You get the job done—and I'm grateful for that.
You don't leave us like an unfinished project on a
workbench. You don't get distracted and forget.
Thank You, Lord! You have started my life, and I know
You will finish the development of my character for
Your good purpose in my life. Create in me integrity,
faith, and joy, Lord, and help me to finish well.

—*Jackie M. Johnson*

Many, O Lord my God,

are the wonders you have done.

The things you planned for us

no one can recount to you;

were I to speak and tell of them,

they would be too many to declare.

PSALM 40:5 NIV

Promise of

Heavenly Treasure

"They sow the wind and they
reap the whirlwind."

Hosea 8:7 nasb

Sowing the Wind

Admit it. Sometimes our jam-packed days leave us feeling as if we're running around like chickens with our heads cut off. From the first drop of morning coffee to the last sip of evening tea, our days reel by in fast motion. The next thing we know, a year has passed. Then two, then three. And what have we done? Where are we?

And why are we running? Why are we constantly moving at warp speed, our feet barely touching the ground as the world around us becomes a blur amid the busyness?

What is the point of our days? Are we chasing after foreign idols, proudly wearing a badge of busyness, worshipping the almighty dollar, determined to keep one step ahead of the Joneses?

That's what the Israelites were doing when Hosea wrote, "They sow the wind and they reap the whirlwind." In sowing the wind, nothing of everlasting value is produced, and we end up with arms filled with temporal nothings.

As followers of Christ, we are to reap righteousness, keeping our eyes on Jesus, for He is our ultimate prize—not that new car, new house, or new wardrobe.

Don't lust for earthly idols that keep you from sowing the right seeds—those of righteousness. Take a deep breath. Take a long walk. Depart from the rat race. Relax in God's arms. Keep your eyes on Christ instead of worldly goods, and you will reap not the earthly whirlwind but heavenly treasure.

—*Donna K. Maltese*

Your only treasures are those

which you carry in your heart.

DEMOPHILUS

Treasures in Heaven

Lord, You are my true treasure. I value all that
You are—holy, wise, loving, and just. You are
mighty and powerful, the giver of life. Help me
to take my eyes off *things* as a source of meaning;
they may be nice and helpful, but inevitably
they fade away. My hope is in You, Lord, and my
fortune to come, in heaven.

—*Jackie M. Johnson*

Every good and perfect gift is from above,
coming down from the Father of the
heavenly lights, who does not change
like shifting shadows.

JAMES 1:17 NIV

The Great Gift Giver

Do you know a true gift giver? We all give gifts on birthdays and at Christmas, when we receive wedding invitations, and when a baby is born. But do you know someone with a real knack for gift giving? She finds all sorts of excuses for giving gifts. She delights in it. A true gift giver has an ability to locate that "something special." When shopping for a gift, she examines many items before making her selection. She knows the interests and preferences, the tastes and favorites of her friends and family members. She chooses gifts they will like—gifts that suit them well.

God is a gift giver. He is, in fact, the Creator of all good gifts. He finds great joy in blessing you. The God who made you certainly knows you by name. He knows your tastes and preferences. He even knows your favorites and your dreams. Most important, God knows your needs.

So in seasons of waiting in your life, rest assured that gifts chosen and presented to you by the hand of God will be worth the wait.

—*Emily Biggers*

If we are children of God, we have a tremendous
treasure in nature and will realize that it is holy
and sacred. We will see God reaching out to us
in every wind that blows, every sunrise and
sunset, every cloud in the sky, every flower that
blooms, and every leaf that fades.

OSWALD CHAMBERS

Hope in God,
Rich in Generosity

I am setting my hope on You today, Lord,
for You provide me with everything to enjoy.
Your treasure of creation—trees, flowers, children,
animals, sunsets, stars—are wonders to my eyes
and a balm to my heart. With You supplying all
that I need, I can do good works, be ready to
share, and thus build up treasures in heaven.
This way of life, enveloped by Your presence,
is the true way. Keep my feet sure on this path.
Take care of me today and through the days to come.

—*Donna K. Maltese*

As for the rich in this present age, charge them. . .

to set their hopes. . .on God, who richly provides us

with everything to enjoy. They are to do good,

to be rich in good works, to be generous and ready

to share, thus storing up treasure for themselves as

a good foundation for the future, so that they may

take hold of that which is truly life.

1 TIMOTHY 6:17–19 ESV

Promise of Joy

I cry aloud to the Lord;

I lift up my voice to the Lord for mercy.

I pour out my complaint before him;

before him I tell my trouble.

Surely you desire truth in the inner parts.

<small>PSALM 142:1–2; 51:6 NIV</small>

Be Real

Writing in a private journal is risky. If someone reads it, the writer is exposed by what and how she wrote. So it is with the psalmists. Their hearts are exposed, showing how very real they were with God. They put on no spiritual face when writing their prayers, thoughts, and songs. They are very real. They complain. They cry out. They vent in anger, weep in remorse, ask deep questions, sing with joy, and dance in celebration. Their honesty before God is refreshing. That is why for so many people, Psalms is their favorite book of the Bible. How gracious of God to include this book for the comfort of His people.

As Psalms demonstrates, God wants genuineness and truth in our hearts. He can handle it. He is not surprised to find anger or questions aimed at Him. Truth sets us free—be honest in examining your heart. See and accept things for what they are. New levels of communion with God are the result of an honest heart, deepening your walk with your Creator. Vibrancy and authentic joy bubble from within a heart that is clean, open, and entwined with God.

—P. J. Lehman

To be a joy-bearer and a joy-giver says
everything, for in our life, if one is joyful,
it means that one is faithfully living for
God, and that nothing else counts;
and if one gives joy to others one is doing
God's work; with joy without and
joy within, all is well.

JANET ERSKINE STUART

God Gives Joy

Oh, giver of all things good, how grateful I am that You have granted me godly happiness. I am truly undeserving of this blessing, but what refreshment it is to turn from the cares of everyday life and be bathed in Your eternal joy! I am humbled when I recall how willingly You gave of Yourself that I might experience this pleasure.

—Rachel Quillin

I pray that God, the source of hope, will fill you completely with joy and peace because you trust in him. Then you will overflow with confident hope through the power of the Holy Spirit.

ROMANS 15:13 NLT

God of Hope

In our busy, fast-paced lives, we may feel exhausted at times. Our culture fosters frenzy and ignores the need for rest and restoration. Constantly putting out fires and completing tasks, working incessantly, we may feel discouraged and disheartened with life. There is more to life than this, isn't there?

Our God of hope says, *"Yes!"* God desires to fill us to the brim with joy and peace. But to receive this gladness, rest, and tranquillity, we need to have faith in the God who is trustworthy and who says, "Anything is possible if a person believes" (Mark 9:23 NLT). We need to place our confidence in God who, in His timing and through us, will complete that task, mend that relationship, or do whatever it is we need. The key to receiving and living a life of hope, joy, and peace is recounting God's faithfulness out loud, quietly in your heart, and to others. When you begin to feel discouraged, exhausted, and at the end of your rope, *stop*; go before the throne of grace and recall God's faithfulness.

—*Tina C. Elacqua*

Let the eternal Truth be your sole
and supreme joy.

Thomas à Kempis

I Will Rejoice

You are with me, dear Jesus. What more could I wish?
Just being with You today makes my heart sing,
and it's a joy no one can steal from me. You have given it
freely, and You want it to be mine. I cherish this treasure,
and I want those around me to experience it, too.
Let my life so exude Your joy that everyone I meet
will desire You, too.

—Rachel Quillin

But may the righteous be glad and rejoice before God;

may they be happy and joyful.

PSALM 68:3 NIV

Promise of Peace

"Come to me, all you who are weary and burdened, and I will give you rest. Take my yoke upon you and learn from me. . .you will find rest for your souls. For my yoke is easy and my burden is light."

MATTHEW 11:28–30 NIV

Lay It at the Cross

Does life sometimes get you down? Often when we experience difficulties that weigh us down, we hear the old adage "Lay it at the cross." But how do we lay our difficulties at the cross?

Jesus gives us step-by-step guidance in how to place our difficulties and burdens at the foot of the cross. First, He invites us to come to Him; those of us who are weary and burdened just need to approach Jesus in prayer. Second, He exchanges our heavy and burdensome load with His easy and light load. Jesus gives us His yoke and encourages us to learn from Him. The word *yoke* refers to Christ's teachings, Jesus' *way* of living life. As we follow His teachings, we take His yoke in humility and gentleness, surrendering and submitting ourselves to His will and ways for our lives. Finally, we praise God for the rest He promises to provide us.

Do you have any difficulties in life, any burdens, worries, fears, relationship issues, finance troubles, or work problems that you need to "lay at the cross"? Jesus says, "Come."

—*Tina C. Elacqua*

All God's glory and beauty come from within,
and there He delights to dwell.
His visits there are frequent, His conversation
sweet, His comforts refreshing,
His peace passing all understanding.

THOMAS À KEMPIS

Calm My Anxious Heart

Lord, I don't want to be anxious about anything, but so often I am. I thank You that You understand. Right now I release my burdens and cares to You. I give You my heavy heart and my flailing emotions. I ask that You calm me, despite all that is happening in my life. As I keep my thoughts, actions, and attitudes centered on Jesus, Your peace comes. I thank You for Your peace that settles on me even when I do not understand.

—*Jackie M. Johnson*

Then she said, "Give me a blessing;
since you have given me the land of the
Negev, give me also springs of water."
So he gave her the upper springs
and the lower springs.

JOSHUA 15:19 NASB

Ask and You Shall Receive

Throughout the Bible, women often appear on the scene as the voice of practicality. Abigail appealed to David's understanding of God; the daughters of Zelophehad petitioned Moses for fairness (Numbers 27:1–8). And here Achsah, the daughter of Caleb, asks her father for water. Caleb had just awarded Achsah and her new husband a generous piece of land, but she knew that in the middle of a desert they needed more than land; they needed water.

In our overwhelming schedules today, as we try to balance all the different pieces of our lives, we should never overlook a very reasonable solution to our need for more time in the day and more hands for the work: Ask for help. It is biblical, practical, and understandable. And, in doing so, we just may be blessed by the kind of help God brings into our lives.

—Ramona Richards

Let my soul take refuge. . .

beneath the shadow of Your wings;

let my heart, this sea of restless waves,

find peace in You, O God.

Augustine

Jesus,
Prince of Peace

Lord, I thank You that I can have a calm
spirit—because You are the Prince of Peace.
Your name, Jesus, has the authority to make fear
and worry flee. Your name has power! You are
called Wonderful Counselor because You freely
give wisdom and guidance. You are the Mighty
God, the One who made the entire world and
keeps it all going. My Everlasting Father, it's Your
love and compassion that sustain me. My Prince
of Peace, I worship and honor You.

—*Jackie M. Johnson*

"*I have told you these things, so that in me you may have peace. In this world you will have trouble. But take heart! I have overcome the world.*"

JOHN 16:33 NIV

Promise of Protection

"*Have I not commanded you?*
Be strong and courageous.
Do not be terrified; do not be discouraged,
for the Lord your God will be
with you wherever you go."

JOSHUA 1:9 NIV

Be Strong and Courageous

In Joshua 1:9 God demands Joshua to "be strong and courageous," a phrase that is repeated five more times in the book of Joshua. When God repeatedly demands something, we would do well to pay attention. But are we listening to God, or are we letting the fears of this world paralyze us?

Many things in this world can terrify us—the state of the economy, terrorist threats, the current crime rate, another car swerving into our lane of traffic—the list goes on and on. But we are to take courage and be strong. We are *commanded* to do so.

Someone has calculated that the words *fear not* appear exactly 365 times in the Bible. How wonderful to have this affirmation available to us every day of the year! Praise God that with Christ the Deliverer in our lives, we are no longer threatened by the world around us. He has overcome all! Now all *we* need to do is believe it!

Believe that God is with you every moment of the day. Believe that He has the power to protect and shield you from the poisonous darts of the evil one. Believe that He has overcome the world. Believe that you have the courage to face the unfaceable. Nothing on this earth can harm you.

—*Donna K. Maltese*

The light of God surrounds me;

The love of God enfolds me;

The power of God protects me;

The presence of God watches over me.

Wherever I am, God is.

UNKNOWN

My Times Are in God's Hands

Lord, I thank You that Your hands are strong and steady. My times are in Your hands—and that's a good place for them to be. In my hands they could fall and break. But not in Yours. Your hands create, Your hands guide and direct, and Your hands hold and comfort. I am secure in every season of my life, knowing that You will protect me and keep me safe. Hand in hand, may we face the future with hope.

—*Jackie M. Johnson*

We can rejoice, too, when we run into problems and trials, for we know that they help us develop endurance. And endurance develops strength of character, and character strengthens our confident hope of salvation.

Darkness into Light

When anything unexpected, painful, or trying comes our way, our first reaction is to run from it. Whether it's an illness, job loss, strained friendship, or even the everyday challenges that sneak up, we want to find the quickest way out.

Imagine a person who is afraid of the dark watching a sunset. The sky darkens and the light fades. Facing her biggest fear, the person attempts to chase after the sun. But the earth is moving too quickly, and no one could ever avoid night completely.

Fortunately, we have a loving God who promises to stay beside us through the darkness. Even though night does come, the quickest way to see the morning is to take God's hand and walk through the hard times. In the morning, the sun rises and the darkness fades, but God is still there.

God never promised that our lives would be easy, but He did promise that He would always be with us—in the darkness and all through the night.

—*Kate E. Schmelzer*

God is with us,
and His power is around us.

CHARLES H. SPURGEON

Calling All Angels

Oh, what a tremendous God You are! You have commanded Your angels to surround me. Right now they are protecting me, guarding me from danger. You will not let anything that is not of Your will touch me. You won't even let me trip over a stone. With Your heavenly host surrounding me, there is no need to fear. Still my rapidly beating heart as I take one breath. . .then another. . .then another, here in Your presence. You are an awesome God. You are *my* God. Thank You for always being there—here—in my heart.

—*Donna K. Maltese*

Our Lord is great, with limitless strength;
we'll never comprehend what he knows and does.

PSALM 147:4–5 MSG

Promise of Rest

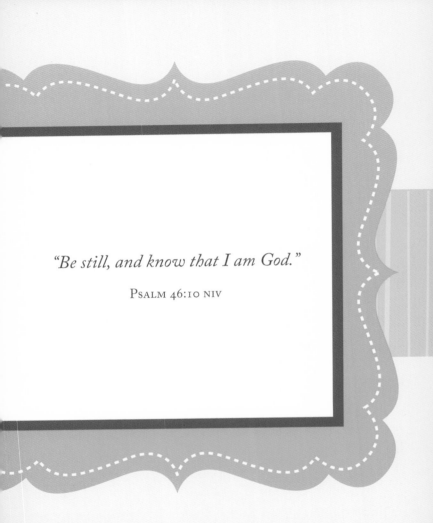

"Be still, and know that I am God."

Psalm 46:10 niv

Be Still

From the minute the alarm clock goes off in the morning, we are busy. Many women rush off to work or begin their tasks around the house without even eating breakfast. Most of us keep hectic schedules, and it is easy to let the day pass by without a moment of peace and quiet.

In Psalm 46:10 the command to *be still* is coupled with the result of *knowing that He is God.* Could it be that to truly recognize God's presence in our lives, we must make time to quiet ourselves before Him?

Sitting quietly before the Lord is a discipline that requires practice. Just as in our earthly relationships, learning to be a good listener as we converse with our heavenly Father is important. If prayer remains one-sided, we will miss out on what He has to say to us.

Although God may not speak to us in an audible voice, He will direct our thinking and speak to our hearts. Stillness allows us to dwell on God's sovereignty, His goodness, and His deep love for us. He wants us to remember that He is God and that He is in control, regardless of our circumstances.

Be still—and know that He is God.

—*Emily Biggers*

Nothing in all creation is so like God as stillness.

Finding Strength

Lord, I am tired and weary. Infuse me with life,
energy, and joy again. I thank You for being my
strength and my delight. I don't have to look to a
bowl of ice cream or to the compliments of a friend
to fill me up on the inside. Steady and constant,
You are my source; You are the One who fills me.
Sustain me, Lord, with the power of Your love so I
can live my life refreshed and renewed.

—*Jackie M. Johnson*

*The Lord God formed man of the dust
of the ground, and breathed into his
nostrils the breath of life.*

Take Five

How would you describe your physical and mental state today? Are you rested and refreshed, or do you feel weary, worn down by the unrelenting demands and pressures of doing life? We tend to think that the longer and harder we work, the more productive we will be. But when we become fatigued spiritually and emotionally, we eventually reach a point of exhaustion.

You *are* in control, and you *can* stop the world from spinning. Even if you know that it is impossible to take a day off, it helps tremendously to make time for a personal time-out.

Pause from whatever you are doing for just a few moments and breathe deeply. Shut your office door, close your eyes, or pause for a second or two in the bathroom. Ask God for a sense of calm and clarity of mind to deal properly with your next assignment. Take time to unwind from a stressful day by a few minutes of "me time" in the car as you drive home. If your commute is short, pull over for a few minutes and let the weight of the day fall off.

Sometimes the most active thing we can do is rest, even if for only a short time.

—*Shanna Gregor*

Spiritual Health

Lord, I need Your times of refreshing in my life.
Bread of Heaven, as You nourish my body with food,
feed my soul with Your words of comfort and life.
May I be filled with Your healing love, joy, and goodness.
I praise You, Father, for providing green pastures, places to
relax and unwind in the Spirit. Please still my heart from
distractions and be the restorer of my soul.

—*Jackie M. Johnson*

When God finds a soul that rests in
Him and is not easily moved,
He operates within it in His own manner.
That soul allows God to do great things within it.
He gives to [it] the key to the treasures He has
prepared for it so that it might enjoy them.
And to this same soul He gives the joy of His presence.

CATHERINE OF GENOA

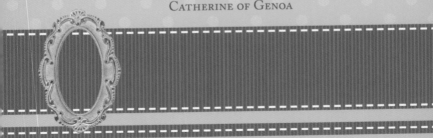